Bibliographical Series
of Supplements to ' British Book News '
on Writers and Their Work

*

GENERAL EDITOR
T. O. Beachcroft

JOYCE CARY

JOYCE CARY

By WALTER ALLEN

PUBLISHED FOR
THE BRITISH COUNCIL
and the NATIONAL BOOK LEAGUE
BY LONGMANS, GREEN & CO., LONDON, NEW YORK, TORONTO

LONGMANS, GREEN & CO. LTD.
6 & 7 Clifford Street, London W.1
Also at Melbourne and Cape Town

LONGMANS, GREEN & CO. INC.
55 Fifth Avenue, New York 3

LONGMANS, GREEN & CO.
215 Victoria Street, Toronto 1

ORIENT LONGMANS LTD.
Bombay, Calcutta, Madras

First published in 1953
Revised edition, 1954

Printed in Great Britain by Benham and Company Limited
Colchester

JOYCE CARY

I

IN a famous passage in the *Biographia Literaria*, Coleridge isolates two opposed modes of the creative activity in their purest and most comprehensive expression. 'While Shakespeare', he says, 'darts himself forth, and passes into all forms of character and passion, the one Proteus of the fire and flood, Milton attracts all forms and things to himself, into unity of his own ideal. All things and modes of action shape themselves anew in the being of Milton; while Shakespeare becomes all things, yet for ever remaining himself.' Coleridge is not making a value-judgement; he is contrasting the objective imagination with the subjective, we might say the extravert as artist with the introvert.

Few poets and novelists are so completely of their type as Shakespeare and Milton; between the two extremes are infinite gradations. Yet if one looks at English fiction during the past thirty years in the light of Coleridge's distinction, it is apparent that it has been predominantly Miltonic, subjective, introvert; so much so that the Shakespearian, objective, extraverted writer stands out with the novelty of the exceptional. He appears old-fashioned, or at least out of step with his time. The neat generalizations we evolve to sum up contemporary writing do not seem to apply to him. And this, perhaps, is the first thing that strikes us when we contemplate the novelist Joyce Cary against the background of his contemporaries. We are immediately aware of his *difference*, and the first difference is that pre-eminently he is 'the one Proteus' of the English novel to-day. Like the poet as seen by Keats, he appears to have 'no identity—he is continually in for and filling some other Body'. So in turn, it seems without the slightest difficulty and with the greatest air of conviction, he becomes an African Negro warrior, an African native clerk from the mission school, an Irish landowner, an evacuee Cockney delinquent boy, a middle-aged domestic servant in prison

5

for theft, a crotchety old lawyer, a painter of genius, the wife of a Radical politician. He is, to put it at the lowest, a superb impersonator, a truly protean actor. This in itself is much; but what gives him a value beyond this is the fact that his novels, taken together, are the expression of a view of life interesting and important in its own right, a view of life so considered and coherent as to be a whole system of belief. His novels are self-contained entities; Cary is as much ' outside ' his work as Flaubert was; so his system of belief is never explicitly stated in his novels, but it can be derived from them, and it is the sub-stratum of their being.

Standing apart from what are usually judged the main tendencies of his time in fiction, Cary stands apart from the majority of living English novelists in the circumstances of his life. He came to the writing of fiction relatively late; his first novel, *Aissa Saved*, did not appear until 1932, when he was forty-four. He was born in Londonderry, in Northern Ireland, in 1888, of a family originally from Devon—he returns to both in his novels. He was an art student in Paris before going up to Oxford, and after Oxford he went to Eastern Europe and took part in the Balkan War of 1912–13, first in a Montenegrin battalion and then with a British Red Cross unit. Then, in 1913, he joined the Nigerian Political Service, serving in the First World War in the campaigns against the Germans in West Africa, until he resumed his duties as magistrate and executive officer in a remote region of Nigeria. He came to literature, then, after a career unlike that of most novelists, a career spent among primitive peoples and largely concerned with government and administration.

Since 1932 he has published thirteen novels, two narrative poems, *Marching Soldier* and *The Drunken Sailor*, two works of political philosophy, *Power in Men* and *Process of Real Freedom*, and two studies of African problems, *The Case for African Freedom* and *Britain and West Africa*. In *The Case for African Freedom* he describes himself as a man who:

after ten years of active, thoughtless and various experience in the world, began, rather late in youth, to ask what it amounted to ; to dig up all his foundations, to find out exactly what they were ; who discovered then, as you might expect, that some of them were mud, some were hollow caves of air, others sand ; and who then slowly and painfully rebuilt them, as far as he could manage the task, as a coherent whole, on which to found a new life and a new mind.

It was from this transvaluation of values following a life largely removed from literary preoccupations that Cary's fiction sprang.

II

Artistic development in the usual sense is absent from Cary's novels. One reason for this comes from his method of work. 'I do not', he has said, 'write one novel at a time. The process is more like collecting. . . . I have a great number of . . . manuscripts in every stage of development.' Yet a general movement may be traced through his work, a movement from the treatment of the comparatively simple theme to that of the much more complex; and in retrospect, his novels seem to fall into four main groups, which may be loosely characterized as the African novels, *Aissa Saved*, *An American Visitor*, *The African Witch*, and *Mister Johnson*; the novels of childhood, *Charley Is My Darling* and *A House of Children*; the novels *Herself Surprised*, *To Be a Pilgrim*, and *The Horse's Mouth*, which relate the history of their time through the individual stories of three characters whose lives to some extent are intertwined; and the novels written since those, *The Moonlight*, *A Fearful Joy*, and *Prisoner of Grace*, in which Cary appears again as the historian of the past seventy years of English life as seen through significant characters. The classification is admittedly very rough, and the list omits *Castle Corner*, which was published during what one thinks of as Cary's African period and which seems to me, despite the extraordinary vividness, through a huge gallery of characters, of its description of Anglo-Irish life and the rise of colonial imperialism in the eighteen-nineties, to be a brilliant failure, an early attempt at the novel of contemporary or near-contemporary history he was to write so successfully a few years later.

All these novels, for all their great variety of scenes, actions, and characters, are of a piece; only Cary could have written them. Each is a metaphorical statement, a statement expressed through images of human beings in action, of his underlying beliefs about the nature of man and the universe, of his philosophy. But the word philosophy may well pull us up short. A man may have the profoundest, most comprehensive and wisest views on the nature of things and still, when he attempts fiction, be a very poor novelist. Novelists and philosophers follow different modes of apprehending reality; which is why novelist-philosophers are so rare. Normally, nothing is so much beside the point in the discussion of a novel as its author's beliefs, for great novels have been written by men whose beliefs have been superficial, absurd, and even ignoble. And the validity or otherwise of Cary's beliefs is not the first thing that concerns us here. What is important now is that his characters, along with the technical means he uses in order to render them in action, all originate in his beliefs about the nature of man. He has stated these beliefs explicitly in his political philosophy; they may equally well be deduced from his fiction.

The characters of every novelist or dramatist, no matter how protean his imagination, bear a family resemblance to one another. This is true even of Shakespeare's. Cary's too are plainly products of the same man's imagination. Black or white, rich or poor, male or female, they have certain outstanding qualities in common. Aissa in *Aissa Saved*; Bewsher and Obai, in *An American Visitor*; Rackham, Judy Coote, Louis Aledai, Schlemm, in *The African Witch*; Jarvis in *Castle Corner*; Mr. Johnson, in the novel of that name; Charley, in *Charley Is My Darling*; Pinto, Delia, Anketel, in *A House of Children*; Sara Munday and Rozzie, in *Herself*

Surprised; Wilcher, in *To Be a Pilgrim*; Jimson, in *The Horse's Mouth*; Aunt Rose and Harry Dawburn, in *The Moonlight*; Tabitha Baskett, Lord Gollan and Bonser, in *A Fearful Joy*; Nimmo, in *Prisoner of Grace*; empire-builders, warriors, clerks, drunken tutors, children, cooks, barmaids, lawyers, painters, spinsters, wives, mistresses, politicians, all the characters that seem typical of Cary are in the grip of what can only be called the creative imagination. Wilcher is in some ways an exception, but he recognizes its power in others, as when he says of his sister Lucy and her husband, Brown, the hellfire-and-damnation evangelist from the working class : ' They were both people of power; life ran in them with a primitive force and innocence. They were close to its springs as children are close, so that its experiences, its loves, its wonders, its furies, its mysterious altruism, came to them as children, like mysteries, and gave them neither peace nor time to fall into sloth or decadence.'

The creative imagination : Cary is its novelist and its celebrant. His characters are impelled by fantasies personal in the deepest sense, unique to each one of them, which must be translated into action. Life about them is, as it were, so much raw material that must be shaped according to their fantasies, which are never seen as fantasies because they are so fundamental to the characters who are moved by them. And the shaping fantasy, creative imagination, is something belonging to man by virtue of his being man. Cary's *Power in Men* begins :

> The weakest child has power and will. Its acts are its own. It can be commanded, but it need not obey. It originates each least movement. It is an independent source of energy which grows with its life and ends only with its death.
> This power is creative. . . .
> This creative power is free. . . .

He goes on : ' Liberty is creation in the act. It is therefore eternal and indestructible.' And more recently, in his broadcast conversation with Lord David Cecil, published as ' The Novelist at Work ', he has spoken of ' this world which is condemned to be free; which is condemned to be free and condemned to live by its imagination '. And the creative action of the imagination is unceasing, continuous, each man ' trying to create a universe which suits his feelings '. Inevitably, since each man is unique and his shaping fantasy unique, his fantasies clash with those of his fellows and, often, with the established order of society, the generally accepted scheme of things. For the individual the consequences may be tragic; equally, from the standpoint of society, they may be comic: in Cary's novels the comic and the tragic are different sides of the one coin.

An important part of Cary's main theme is the creative imagination of the individual in action in conflict with those of others or with authority. To begin with, in his African novels, he dramatized this conflict as the conflict between races and colours, between modes of being alien to each side and more or less incomprehensible to it. We are shown in these novels primitive peoples confronted with a new and almost wholly unintelligible civilization, taking what they want from the white man's religion and way of life and making of it a new thing satisfying to them but quite baffling to the white administrators and missionaries. One thinks especially of the mission scenes in these novels: the native who has ' got ' Christianity does not become as a result any more like his white Christian mentors; indeed, his interpretation of Christianity may appear to them as a blasphemous parody. But the ' Christianized ' native is in conflict not only with his saddened white teachers but also with his fellows who are still pagan and with those who are Moslem. The African world described, then, is one in which everyone is at cross-purposes with everyone else. Inevitably, the tragic and the comic are inextricably mingled.

As renderings and interpretations of primitive psychology, these novels are among the best we have in English, and an index of Cary's success in them is the fact that the white characters are revealed as no less essentially strange than the black: Cary enters the minds of both with an impartial gusto and sympathy, as E. M. Forster, for example, in *A Passage to India*, does not enter the minds of his English characters. The Resident Magistrate Rudbeck, in *Mister Johnson*, is just as much caught by compulsive fantasy, the fantasy of himself as a builder of roads—there are all sorts of good reasons for building roads, but in his case they are all rationalizations of an overmastering desire to build roads for the sake of building roads—as is the infinitely comic, infinitely pathetic Johnson himself, the clerk from the mission school who identifies himself with the white man's way of life and, full of lordly exuberance and expansiveness, combines the ingenuousness of a child with the myth-making mind of a poet—to his ultimate catastrophe, death at the hands of the white man's justice.

It was perhaps a natural step for Cary to take, to pass from the representation of primitives to the representation of children. It was wholly typical of him that when he did so he should write in rapid succession two novels depicting children placed in utterly dissimilar circumstances. The first was *Charley Is My Darling*. The second, *A House of Children*, I suspect is autobiographical in origin : it is presented as the author's memories of his early boyhood among a large upper-middle-class family living on the north-west coast of Ireland during the eighteen-nineties. There is no attempt to re-create childhood in itself; what are admirably caught are the changes, the growth, the discontinuities, even the regressions of childhood when looked back upon from adult life, and, above all, the sudden sense of glory which, however intermittently, illuminates every childhood at some time. It is an enchanting novel.

Most of the characters of *Charley Is My Darling* are London slum children evacuated to Devon in the early days of the recent war. Charley Brown, a boy of fifteen, as much as any character in Cary's world, suffers from that 'hunger of the imagination', in Dr. Johnson's tremendous phrase, 'which preys incessantly on life'. His imagination, in response to the life about him, is constantly setting him ideals of behaviour which he must try to live up to; and it is from sheer exuberance of imagination working in unfamiliar circumstances that he drifts into what I suppose must be called juvenile delinquency. The end of the novel is near-tragedy, poignantly so; but it is reached through episodes of comedy which, though often tender and moving, become progressively wilder almost to the point of farce. Yet wild as the comedy is, we do not doubt either the reality of the characters or the truth of the situations they find themselves in. One reason for this lies in the particular methods Cary has evolved for rendering character in action, methods rooted in his philosophy.

III

As a novelist, Cary is generally spoken of as being much more traditional than most of the major novelists of our time. This does not mean that he practises his art precisely as the eighteenth-century novelists or the Victorians did theirs. Inasmuch as he renders human beings as unique individuals caught in their own fantasies, and often at the extremes of individuality, as Jimson is in *The Horse's Mouth*, it is understandable that he should draw characters in the minute particulars of eccentricity such as we find in Dickens. Again, in the furious pace of his comedy, in his later novels especially, as in his high spirits, he has obvious kinship with Smollett. Then, the first-person narration of *Herself Surprised*, and the overtones of the device, hark back to Defoe's *Moll Flanders*. Yet *The Horse's Mouth* could scarcely have been written by someone who had not absorbed into his own artistic being the 'laboratory' work of James Joyce; and if there are affinities with Defoe, Smollett, and Dickens, those with D. H. Lawrence are hardly less plain.

Indeed, one of Cary's most considerable achievements is his success in grafting on to the trunk of our traditional fiction, with its stress on story, action, and broadly conceived character, technical devices first used in the experimental novels of this century, by Joyce, Lawrence, and Virginia Woolf particularly in their various ways. In classic English fiction for the most part—there are obvious exceptions, Richardson and Sterne the most conspicuous—the action of the novel is as it were completed before the reader picks up the book and reads. The action lies in the past, and the novelist's role is that of reporter of events already over ; and as he reports his closed sequence of events he feels himself free to comment as he wishes on the action, to generalize and moralize on it, even to advise the reader which characters to admire, which to deplore. The reader is therefore at a distance from the characters of classic fiction : the author is in between. With Joyce and Virginia Woolf, and in a different way with Lawrence, this is not so ; their aim was precisely to break down the old barriers between reader and character. The methods differ with each writer, but always the reader is taken right inside the minds of the characters ; plunged into the stream of consciousness of Mr. Bloom, given the freedom of Mrs. Bloom's drifting unspoken soliloquies, made to feel the very sense of outrage and defilement Aaron feels when his pocket is picked in *Aaron's Rod*, invited to share the sensibility and fine discriminations of Mrs. Ramsay as she contemplates her husband, children, and guests, and the lighthouse they may or may not visit. These novelists were intent on rendering the moment of consciousness in itself; in their different ways they give us close-ups of consciousness ; and as we read them we find ourself for much of the time—occasionally the author has to provide us with the equivalents of stage-directions—in what may be called a continuous present.

We experience much the same thing when we read Cary, at any rate after his early novels : while reading, we are at the cutting-edge of the present. Cary is incomparable among living novelists at pinning down the sense of life at the actual moment of being lived. He succeeds in capturing this even in his first-person novels, which, as

fictitious autobiography, must be retrospective. Take the
following passage from *A House of Children* :

> We shrieked together in joyful terror. We were growing
> drunk with expectation, which was increasing all the time. For
> in us children it was a pure passion and never checked itself for
> reason. It burned on its own fuel, so that its size had no
> relation to its source; we were often in a fever for something
> so trifling that we had forgotten it before it arrived. All
> one day one would live in the sense of something to come; it
> would be with one during lessons, bathing, digging, meals,
> until at last, getting into bed, one would notice it particularly
> and say: 'But what am I expecting ?' Then one would
> discover that it had been doughnuts for tea, already eaten, but
> with no sense of fulfilment. The expectation had flowed over
> the fact as time runs over the apple flowers before one can grasp
> the spring. But with us, it was like an eddy on a strong tide.
> A specific anticipation was no more than a fresh bubble in the
> stream of our hope, rushing towards fulfilment. . . . We were
> not the pathetic deceived children of the story-books, entering
> step by step the prison shades of grown-up disillusionment, we
> were confident of happiness because we had had it before. Our
> several expectations were sometimes not realized, but that was
> usually because our whole expectation was being renewed
> every hour. We didn't notice the disappointments because our
> minds were full of something else, something new, something
> interesting.

The passage expresses a truth about the nature of children ;
but its immediate relevance now is as a key to Cary. For
Cary, to be alive is to be in a state of continuous creation,
and this is why he must seek always to snare the moment of
living itself. But simultaneously he has to do something
else, something which on the face of it should defeat the end
of snaring the moment in itself. I have said his novels are
metaphorical statements of his system of beliefs. These
metaphorical statements have to be generalized. Two
quotations will show how he does this. The first is from
Mister Johnson : the hero is giving a highly successful party :

> Johnson walks through the crowd in his best white suit, new

patent leathers, and a pearl-grey hat, exactly like Gollop's, on the side of his head. His face shines with sweat and his mouth is spread perpetually in an enormous grin. Every moment he shouts out some joke, some greeting, takes a step with the dancers, miming their steps, throws a ball for the juggler or, all by himself, makes a little song and dance expressing some impulse of delight, pride, or of hospitable affection for mankind.

It is, incidentally, a good example of the way Cary's empathic imagination works, his ability to feel himself into his characters in their changing moods and emotions, physical behaviour, gesture. Indeed, it is just Johnson's gestures that Cary is at pains to imitate; they are in a sense the generalization itself.

The second quotation is from *Charley Is My Darling*. It describes the end of that momentous day when Charley takes his gang to the cinema, an excursion involving the thefts both of a motor-car and of a handbag. The gang is splitting up for the night. Ginger goes first; ' Good night Liz ', he says.

Lizzie does not answer. They watch Ginger stroll into the shadow of the tall house, towards the back door. They hear it open and shut, and they still stand looking towards the house. Liz sighs suddenly.

' Poor Gingurr. I wish I'd said good night to him.'

' I dunno.' Charley turns away.

' E's all right', Harry says. ' E can go in wen e likes and no one says a word to im.'

' Funny ow e got stuck in the cafee—e was shy.'

' Ginger—e aint shy.'

' I like Gingurr—I do wish I'd said good night to him ', Liz sighs again. . ' Poor Gingurr.'

As usual with this expression of pity she seems to be expressing an emotion much wider and much more deeply felt than a passing sympathy with the object mentioned. Children use the same tone, when, on the loss of a doll or a boat, they say: ' Poor doll, poor boat.' They do not pity the doll or the boat so much as wonder, sometimes with curiosity, sometimes fear, at the circumstances within which dolls and boats can be so helplessly smashed.

When such vivid descriptions of character in action are combined with the swift, glancing generalization, the accuracy and insight of which we always accept, we see the character as with a double vision. There is the Negro Johnson, the girl Lizzie, caught while in motion as by a film camera, and there is the generalization like a shadow behind the character, but the shadow not precisely of the character itself, rather of all children, of all sketchily westernized Negroes like Johnson; so that in the behaviour of the specific character, acutely defined though it is, is the behaviour, the development and experience, of the whole class of beings to which the specific character belongs.

Generalization is part of Cary's way of creating character and giving it significance. Yet we never feel his generalizations as shocking intrusions on the action as we do the moral judgements of Thackeray or, at times, George Eliot. In the two quotations above, what ' carries ' his generalizations is the use of the historic present tense. Now almost by definition, the historic present, so often employed by French novelists, rarely succeeds in English; ninety-nine times out of a hundred it seems artificial, unnatural. It does not in Cary, partly, I think, because of the speed of his narrative. He is like a radio commentator of genius who rapidly, almost breathlessly, describes what he sees and interpolates his comment on the action at the very moment of the action; so that comment and generalization become part of the description, part of the total rendering of the scene. Comment, as it were, appears as a spontaneous response.

Cary uses the historic present tense, or a modification of it, in *Mister Johnson*, *Charley Is My Darling*, and *A Fearful Joy*. The last is especially interesting in this respect because of the complexity of the subject-matter to which the device is applied. By comparison, the earlier novels were novels of a simple situation; in *A Fearful Joy* Cary's role is that of the novelist as historian of his own times. He interprets the history of England during the past sixty years as it impinges on his heroine, Tabitha Baskett. A girl in the eighteen-nineties, she is seduced by an engaging scoundrel named Bonser, a young man who lives by his wits and deserts her when she is pregnant. She passes into the protection of a business man who is one of the patrons of the literary and artistic movement of the 'nineties. On his death she marries a new-rich millionaire, an engineer whose ambition is to make an aeroplane that will fly. When he dies, she meets Bonser again; they marry and together keep a seaside hotel and then a roadhouse in the Midlands. Through her children she experiences further social change, so that by the end of the novel she contains the social history of sixty years.

A Fearful Joy is a presentation of change, of the ceaseless striving for novelty that Cary sees as one outcome of the creative imagination. It is not until we have finished the novel and pondered over it that we realize that the change described is largely the result of changes in mechanical transport. For Tabitha herself, the fact of change is something known only after the event, when its reality is brought home to her by other people, as in the following passage, in the year 1900, after her protector, Sturge, the impressario of the Aesthetic Movement, has died:

> And this new age is present to everybody's imagination as something quite clearly divided from the old, not only by the magic figures oo, but by war and the death of the old queen. . . .
>
> Everyone expects newness in art, law, politics, morals; and history itself is renewed from day to day. Enterprising young men, looking for a new field of exploration, have already discovered the Nineties, and Sturge's obituaries, written, as always of the dead, with an historical bias, have placed him and his clique as important figures of that epoch. Boole, at forty-seven, is a living relic of antiquity. When, therefore, he cries to all comers, ' Let me introduce you to Mrs. Bonser, of *The Bankside*, *chère amie* of Bunsurge ', glances directed at

Tabitha are full of approval as well as of curiosity. She is
soon surrounded by men.

' How do you do, Mrs. Bonser. Did you really know
Beardsley ? '

' No, I'm afraid I only met him once.' Tabitha's voice shows
that she does not value Beardsley very highly.

' Mrs. Bonser, excuse me——.' An eager youth accosts her.
' I've been *so* longing to meet you. I'm engaged on a thesis
about the aesthetic movement.'

' But was it really a movement ? ' Tabitha looks with sad
enquiry at the enthusiast. ' Was it really important ? '

' Enormously important. One of our great revolutions, it
brought down the Victorian bastille.' And delighted by the
very idea of this destruction, he draws a picture of heroes going
out to war against tyranny; of Morris routing the money
grubbers, Pater and Symons undermining a philistine morality,
Sturge and Boole releasing imprisoned souls from dark oubli-
ettes.

' But Mr. Sturge was a churchman ', Tabitha says, ' and he
greatly admired the old queen.'

' Now that is a most interesting point '. . . .

Tabitha has no historical bias, which is the result of the
creative imagination working on the past; she is the inno-
cent, uncomprehending present to which things happen un-
awares. She is, as it were, always at the present moment of
time : open the novel wherever you like and it is to-day,
and to-morrow—the next page—is also to-day. What is
caught is the flow of time itself, and this gives a compel-
ling immediacy to Tabitha's experiences. The effect of the
novel is of a series of cartoons drawn with great vigour and
speed, the characters, apart from Tabitha and Bonser,
sketched in boldly rather than developed in detail. So to
exhibit changing social history in fiction, the social history of
a complex period, is an intellectual feat. If *A Fearful Joy* is
less successful than the earlier *To Be a Pilgrim* and *The Horse's
Mouth* it is, I think, because Tabitha is less interesting in her
own right than Wilcher and Jimson ; it is her role to be pas-
sive, and she is not, as they are, transfigured by any abiding

values for which she may stand. It is Bonser, her first seducer, last husband and only love, who steals the book whenever he appears. A blackmailer, a fraud, a womanizer, a drunkard, he remains one of Cary's most lavishly comic creations, for he is redeemed—and the reader's moral judgement inhibited—by his vitality, his sheer delight in living. It is Tabitha's love for him that is the fearful joy of the title. It is the essence of the characters one thinks of as typically Cary's that they enhance life. In a note to his poem *The Drunken Sailor*, he has written: 'There is nothing sure, nothing dependable, but the spirit of life itself and its invincible desperation which, among the cruelty of circumstance that is the form and effect of its real being, begets itself for ever in newness and innocence eternal delight.' Bonser is a manifestation of the invincible desperation of life and so, despite his rogueries, holds Tabitha always in thrall. 'He brought me to life again,' she thinks after his death; 'it was like a resurrection of the dead.' And in the last analysis his rogueries are beside the point.

IV

Cary has another way of achieving the sense of the creative moment itself with the almost simultaneous generalization upon it: the use of first-person narration. It is here that his ability to feel himself into character, so that he becomes the character telling the story, is seen at its fullest. He has used first-person narration in the related novels *Herself Surprised*, *To be a Pilgrim*, and *The Horse's Mouth*, and in his most recent work, *Prisoner of Grace*. *Herself Surprised* is the first novel, as Cary has said,

> of a trilogy which was designed to show three characters, not only in themselves but as seen by each other. The object was to get a three-dimensional depth and force of character. One character was to speak in each book and describe the other two as seen by that person. Sara, the woman in a woman's world, was to see Wilcher and Jimson in that world, in relation to her

own life and her own fortunes.   She was to recall their history
and the history of the times, as part of her own history.   In
practice this scheme, for technical reasons, did not come off.

The result was not a trilogy in the sense of *The Forsyte Saga*
or Ford Madox Ford's Tietjens books, but rather three novels
the stories of which touch at certain points, the link between them all being the character of Sara Munday, the
narrator of *Herself Surprised*.   The three novels, then, com-
pose a group rather than a sequence.

They are probably Cary's finest work to date.   It is, to
say the least, a performance of extraordinary virtuosity that
in successive novels he should have assumed so completely
such diverse personalities as Sara Munday, Mr. Wilcher, and
Gully Jimson.   *Herself Surprised*, the story of Sara and her
associations with Jimson and Wilcher, is one of the most
delightful of modern novels, as Sara is one of the most
delightful of modern heroines.   She recalls, in the warmth
and simplicity of her feelings and in the innocence of her
sensuality, Renoir's nudes.   She is writing her story in prison,
in a state of repentance.   Like Moll Flanders in the novel
of Defoe, which *Herself Surprised* often reminds us of, she
thinks of her life as a moral object-lesson.   A cook, she
has married her employer's son and become a wealthy
woman, and then, after his death, become the mistress first of Jimson, and later, as his housekeeper, of the
elderly lawyer Mr. Wilcher, whose property she has been
convicted of stealing.   She is woman in her twin-role of
mother and mistress; despite her good intentions and her
early religious education, she is incapable of resisting the
demands that man, the male child, makes on her.   If she
cannot square her behaviour with her sincerely held religious beliefs it is because they cannot in the nature of things be
squared.   In her own eyes she is a sinner; but to the reader
her life is a hymn of praise to creation and the Creator.

Along with *Mister Johnson* and *A House of Children*, *Herself Surprised* seems to me the most perfect of Cary's novels.
But perfection in art commonly goes with a relative simpli-

city in theme and treatment. Cary has noted that he ' cut
out history and art in Sara's book ' because ' when I let Sara
talk about art and history I found that she lost something of
her quality and force; the essential Sara was diluted '.
Compared with the two later novels of the group, Sara's
book is on a small scale. If hers is Cary's most perfect novel,
To Be a Pilgrim and *The Horse's Mouth* are his richest in
complexity and his most authoritative as expressions of his
attitude to life. The authority in each comes from the
strength and freshness, the three-dimensional solidity, of the
main character, the narrator.

It is difficult to know which to admire the more as a creative triumph, Wilcher in *To Be a Pilgrim* or Jimson in *The
Horse's Mouth*. On the face of it, Jimson is the more striking, for here Cary achieves the almost impossible, a convincing representation of artistic genius. Jimson as we meet
him is an old and battered man just out of prison; a man for
whom the visible world exists in an almost overpowering
intensity, which he transmits to the reader in a completely
idiosyncratic idiom of speech, extravagant, rhetorical,
slangy, as though he were the child at once of James Joyce
and William Blake. Blake, indeed, is his great exemplar,
the Prophetic Books his nearest thing to a bible. Like
Blake, he is a visionary painter whose work is wildly un-
fashionable; but he lives wholly for his painting, and though
always stricken with poverty and engaged in ingenious and
near-criminal schemes for obtaining money, he keeps all
the time his integrity as a painter.

We see the world as Jimson sees it. Through him, indeed, Cary creates a whole world, eccentric perhaps, but
still a genuine image of the real one. *The Horse's Mouth* is
certainly Cary's most sustained effort in comedy, and to
match the speed and vigour of the writing and its author's
ability to keep it going, one would have to go back as far
as *Peregrine Pickle*. At times Jimson's adventures are ludi-
crous, almost to slapstick farce, though we must remember
that it is Jimson himself, not a stickler for fact, who is nar-

rating them. But the extravagance of the comedy does not make for unreality : it is an expression of the whole man, and the whole man's continual creation of the world he lives in. In spirit, *The Horse's Mouth* is Cary's most eighteenth-century novel : Jimson is really the rogue-hero, looking for a fine wall to paint on as the eighteenth-century rogue-hero looked for a wealthy woman to gull. The comedy depends for its effect on its mounting intensity and duration, and space forbids quotation ; otherwise one would delight in transcribing the wonderful account of Jimson's occupancy of Sir William Beeder's flat and his wrecking and stripping of it in order to paint the mural of the raising of Lazarus that Sir William has not commissioned ; and the masterly climax of the novel, in which Jimson and his young disciples furiously paint a wall of a building the local authorities are even then busy demolishing as unsafe.

Striking as Jimson is, the character of Wilcher seems to me in essentials the greater feat, as I find *To Be a Pilgrim* more profound and on a vaster scale than *The Horse's Mouth.* Wilcher is a true original : there is no other character like him in the range of our fiction. He is an old man, aware that he is regarded by the young as an old fogy. He has played second fiddle all his life, ministering as a lawyer to his elder brothers and sisters, men and women more vital than himself, men and women of action. He is pedantic and fussy, personally a little ridiculous, and he knows it :

> We were sailing in his cranky little boat, a pursuit which causes me acute misery. For wet, especially in the seat, always gave me rheumatism ; the motion of a boat, even on a calm day, made me ill ; the necessity of continually getting up and moving across to the other side of the boat, and ducking my head under the boom, at the risk of my hat, broke up every conversation and exasperated me extremely ; and, finally, I could conceive nothing more stupid than to proceed by zigzags, from nowhere to nowhere, for the sake of wasting a fine afternoon. Neither, if I may mention such a point, though it is probably unimportant, have I ever been able to understand why there was

no accommodation provided on small yachts, for things like sticks and umbrellas; whereas land conveyances, such as gigs and even governess carts, always have a basket designed for their proper storage and protection.

Moreover, as we see him in the journal he is writing—and the novel is really his journal—he is a little cracked, an old man on the verge of senility; an old man whose emotional life has been so repressed that it is now breaking out in ungovernable tendencies towards indecent exposure, so that he has to be kept under restraint by his family. At the same time, and this is perfectly clear throughout, he is a man of real intellect and a man of real religious faith.

In *To Be a Pilgrim*, Cary handles three stories at once. In his journal Wilcher is concerned with his own immediate problem, of how to escape the restraint he is under and run away to rejoin and marry his housekeeper-mistress Sara, who feels only pity for the comic, inhibited, fierce old man; he is also concerned, first in a spirit of hostile scrutiny, with the lives of his niece, a doctor, who is looking after him, and her husband, a nephew, who is struggling to bring the family estate at Tolbrook into cultivation again; and then, at the same time, he is consciously reliving his past, exploring his relations with his parents, brothers, and sisters in order to discover the sources of their strength and his failure. It is here that the novel becomes the magnificent evocation it is of English history from the eighteen-nineties to 1939 from the standpoints of political Liberalism and religious nonconformity—the Protestant position at its most intransigent. Wilcher's brother Edward has been a Liberal politician of daring and distinction; his brother Bill a soldier; his sister Lucy the wife of an itinerant evangelist. All were people of force and power; Wilcher himself is not, but he is a man of imagination, and as he relives his life in his journal he brings his family to life again in all its strength and sense of obligation.

Technically, the organization of *To Be a Pilgrim* is brilliantly skilful. The three stories are told in such a way that each is set off and given added significance by the others; and all are bound together, fused into one, by the darting generalizations, the constant reinterpretation of experience, of Wilcher. By the end of the novel we have realized that the house at Tolbrook, with Ann, Wilcher's doctor-niece, writing her father's biography in what was his study, and Robert her husband using the threshing machine in the great saloon, among the Adam panelling, under the Angelica Kaufmann ceiling, is a symbol of England itself; a more successful one, it seems to me, because more comprehensive, than Forster's similar identification of a house with England in *Howard's End*.

This brings us to what is fundamental to both *To Be a Pilgrim* and *The Horse's Mouth*. Here the title of the former is highly relevant; it is from Bunyan's great hymn:

> Who would true valour see
>   Let him come hither;
> One here will constant be,
>   Come wind, come weather.
> There's no discouragement
> Shall make him once relent
> His first avowed intent
>   To be a pilgrim.

Bunyan, with his direct intuition of the presence of God, his assurance that all power is from Him, and his insistence that no one and nothing, priest or ritual, should be allowed to come between him and God, stands as an archetype of the English Protestant or Nonconformist. When the great nineteenth-century Nonconformist newspaper editor, W. T. Stead, referred to God as ' the Senior Partner ', from whom he got his instructions direct, he was expressing a conviction similar to Bunyan's. Gully Jimson's references to God are even more familiar than Stead's, but he is no less directly God-inspired, and it is the knowledge of this that is ultimately the sanction of his behaviour.

The Protestant or Nonconformist tradition, though its manifestations change from generation to generation, has been one of the most potent and formative in English life, in politics no less than in religion. Cary's system of beliefs is central to that tradition and in his fiction, in *To Be a Pilgrim* and *The Horse's Mouth* above all, he has re-stated it for our time. D. H. Lawrence, who was brought up in religious dissent and remained essentially in dissent all his life, used to say, according to Aldous Huxley, ' I don't feel it *here*', pressing his hands to his solar plexus. In the last analysis, all Protestantism, Nonconformity, begins with the hands pressed on the solar plexus and the ' I don't feel it *here* ', for, in the last analysis, his own existence, his own deepest feelings, are all that any man can be sure of. Often the Nonconformist will appear a hypocrite, as he did to Fielding and Smollett and Dickens, and often he will appear mad, as Blake did. Both are the consequences of his awareness that he is ' condemned to freedom ' and that responsibility is his and no one else's. The burden he feels called to bear, simply by being man, is such as to be endurable only so long as he has faith. Their characters' abiding faith is what gives *To Be a Pilgrim* and *The Horse's Mouth* the special dimension in which they have their being.

It is the quality of Jimson's faith, his unquestioning certainty that he must live and paint according to the light of his intuitions, without regard to the cost in material success, that makes him so much more than a mere eccentric and gives his vision of society, as we see it through his eyes, its value. Jimson shows us an aspect of English working-class life that has rarely had adequate recognition, that perpetual and fructifying ferment of nonconformity, religious and political, among the relatively self-educated. We see it at work among Jimson's friends, Mr. Plant the philosopher, Mr. Ollier the postman, members of tiny societies meeting in back rooms to discuss or reform the universe. They are cranks, but cranks in the tradition of George Fox and Bunyan, Blake, Robert Owen and Keir Hardie. They are not cranks to Jimson; and though the reader may see in him the eternal irresponsible artist, the artist who decides that art is enough for a man to live by, without acquiring other loyalties, to Mr. Plant and his friends he is perfectly normal, for they know that religion takes men in diverse ways and that painting is as natural and proper a mode of religious experience and expression as any other.

In *To Be a Pilgrim*, Wilcher's intuitions are intermittent. Temperamentally, he is a conservative, inclined to take the letter for the spirit. Much of the time he is the pettifogger his sister accuses him of being. Faith comes to him through the living example of others. But he too is a pilgrim. Early on in the novel, he asks himself: ' Why do I ever forget that the glory of my land is also the secret of life, to see at every sunrise, a new horizon ? Why do I ever forget that every day is a new landfall in a foreign land, among strangers ? ' And at the very end, in a wonderful apostrophe of England, he takes up this note again :

> The truth must be confessed, that I am an old fraud, and that I have deceived myself about my abilities. I thought I could be an adventurer like Lucy and Edward; a missionary. I shouted the pilgrim's cry, democracy, liberty, and so forth, but I was a pilgrim only by race. England took me a few stages of her journey. Because she could not help it. She, poor thing, was born upon the road, and lives in such a dust of travel that she never knows where she is.
> ' Where away England, steersman answer me ?
> We cannot tell. For we are all at sea.'
> She is the wandering Dutchman, the pilgrim and scapegoat of the world. Which flings its sins upon her as the old world heaped its sins upon the friars. Her lot is that of all courage, all enterprise; to be hated and abused by the parasite. But, and this has been one of the exasperating things in my life, she isn't even aware of this hatred and jealousy which surrounds her and, in the same moment, seeks and dreads her ruin. She doesn't notice it because she looks forward to the road. Because she is free. She stands always before all possibility, and this is the youth of the spirit. It is the life of the faithful who say, ' I am ready. Anywhere at any time.'

In the end, then, the Nonconformist, Protestant spirit, which is one aspect of the creative imagination that eternally shapes things anew, is equated with the spirit of England herself.

In his most recent novels, *The Moonlight*, *A Fearful Joy*, *Prisoner of Grace*, and *Except the Lord*, Cary dramatizes themes that form part of the whole of *To Be a Pilgrim*. *A Fearful Joy* has already been discussed. *The Moonlight* takes up the problem of the clash of generations and the changing position over women during sixty years. The novel is told in the third person, but again three stories are kept going at once and the lives of the daughters of an upper-class Victorian family are re-created in depth. *The Moonlight* is memorable as a study in the change in women's attitudes to sex and romantic love and as a study also of what Cary has called ' the injustice risked by everyone who accepts responsibility for government ' : Rose, who accepts reponsibility for her sisters and takes on the role almost of father and mother combined, is in the end hated by them all and poisoned by Ella, the weakest of them and the most rebellious, the one she has been at most pains to protect. This novel is also distinguished by a much increased visual intensity in Cary's style, as though, having in the previous book assumed the character of Gully Jimson, he had afterwards retained his painter's eye.

In *Prisoner of Grace*, Cary goes back to the examination of the working of the creative imagination, this time in politics ; and the creative imagination is shown as synonymous with the religious imagination. Chester Nimmo, a Radical politician, begins his career during the South African War, as a pacifist ; in 1914, a Cabinet Minister, he is the leader of the militant section of the British Government. His principles appear to change, but his self-assurance never does. Whatever he does is right because he regards himself as divinely inspired ; his political intuitions, however convenient they may be to him personally, he attributes to God. This confidence of inspiration gives him his authority : he is in a state of grace. It is his wife Nina, who narrates the story, who is the prisoner of grace. She is an unwilling prisoner, for, of a higher social position than Nimmo, she has been forced to marry him by her aunt, the young politician's patron, when discovered pregnant by her cousin Jim Latter. But however much she may love Latter and however much she may criticize Nimmo and his actions, for her values are not political, she cannot escape him; she always, as D. H. Lawrence might have put it, recognizes and responds to the god in him. And she knows he is not a hypocrite, whatever he may seem: he is simply immersed in the political life.

As a study of the politician in action, *Prisoner of Grace* is masterly, and when one compares it with other political novels in English, even with Disraeli's, one sees it is unique in its profundity. It is as though we have for the first time the truth about the quintessential politician, the man for whom politics is a way of life and a vocation in the same dedicated sense as art may be for the artist or religion for the priest. Nimmo himself is a creation of tremendous power; as with Jimson, one feels with him that one is in the presence of a force of nature. And Cary quite triumphantly overcomes the obvious difficulties that faced him in this novel. We know very well what the actual history of the decades before and after the First World War was; but in the most uncanny way Cary seems to supplement it. We know very well who the great historic figures of the times were— Campbell-Bannerman, Balfour, Lloyd George, Asquith, Churchill; it is a proof of his author's achievement that Nimmo, as a fictitious character, is still thoroughly convincing when we recall them.

Prisoner of Grace is the first of an as yet incomplete trilogy of novels; but the second book, *Except the Lord*, has already appeared. It is presented in the form of Chester Nimmo's autobiography, written when he is an old man. It does not, however, reproduce the events described in *Prisoner of Grace*, but recounts Nimmo's story before he met Nina. It shows Cary at his gravest and most austere. The exuberance is severely curbed, and comedy is almost entirely absent. It is a very packed novel, a slice of working-class social history in the Devon of the last decades of the nine-teenth century; and it has many memorable characters, notably Nimmo's father, an old soldier who combines farm-labouring with his vocation as pastor of a small nonconform-ist sect preaching the imminence of the Second Coming, and Nimmo's sister Georgina, one of Cary's most striking representations of children, a *farouche* child whose sense of responsibility and love for her family are expressed through a sort of baffled, indignant criticism of them. But packed though the novel is, and rich in the quality of felt life, everything is subordinated to the theme of the religious nature of man as manifest in the direct intercourse of man with God which is fundamental to nonconformity. *Except the Lord* is Cary's most explicit rendering of the Noncon-formist, Protestant spirit; and it is this very explicitness and directness that give the novel its power and authority.

One understands that the third volume of the trilogy will be written from the point of view of Jim Latter, Nina Nimmo's lover.

V

Our approach to contemporary writers differs from our approach to writers of the past. We are too close to our contemporaries, not only in time but in feelings, assump-tions, fears, and hopes, to be able to see them clearly and whole. We share a world with them, and in a way the writers of the past are not, they are part of ourselves. So to ask of a contemporary whether he will be read in the future or what his stature will be in the eyes of posterity is to ask the wrong questions, questions which in any case cannot be answered. The proper question is: Is he good for us now, and in what way?

We shall not demand of him qualities he does not profess to have; nor, if we are wise, shall we use him as a means by which to denigrate his fellows in the art he practises: one of the great virtues of art is its variety, and what we value in any artist is the sense we have of his uniqueness, the strong impression that the imaginary world he creates is special to him, the expression of one individual mind. So, where Cary is concerned, I do not grumble because his novels in the main lack the particular aesthetic quality of form that we find in the work of novelists in the tradition of Jane Austen and Henry James, much as I appreciate it in those novelists; it is in fact doubtful whether it is ever in the power of the extravert novelist to give us this.

For myself, I value first in Cary the emphatic power of his genius, his protean nature which enabled him, in his African novels, for example, most vividly to body forth the clash not so much of colour but the modes of being underneath the difference of colours. Then, accompanying the empathic imagination, is his exuberance of creation, not a common quality in the English novel to-day, which seems to reproduce, no less, the ' daedal dance ' of life itself. This exuberance cannot be separated from the comprehensiveness of his vision, which has enabled to bring into his fiction a larger area of English life than any other living writer.

But fundamental to everything else is the nature of his vision. Cary has been described by a wit as the Protestant answer to Graham Greene: it would be as true to say that he is the English retort to the Existentialist writers, whether Christian or atheist; though it arises from sources very different from theirs, his view of life in its implications is just as Existential. But it is a very English Existentialism, and if, as I think is true, England and the English cannot be understood except by reference to the working of the Protestant, Nonconformist spirit, then a reading of Cary, of all living novelists, is essential to the understanding of the English. His great value for us now is that he has used all the recources of his art and talent to re-interpret in fiction an enduring tradition in our life and feeling, one without which England and the English would be very different from what they are.

JOYCE CARY

A

Select Bibliography

(Place of publication London, unless stated otherwise)

Collected Edition:
  The Carfax Edition (1951 continuing).
  Each novel with a preface by the author.

Separate Works:
  AISSA SAVED (1932). *Novel.*
  AN AMERICAN VISITOR (1933). *Novel.*
  THE AFRICAN WITCH (1936). *Novel.*
  CASTLE CORNER (1938). *Novel.*
  MISTER JOHNSON (1939). *Novel.*
  POWER IN MEN (1939). *Political Science.*
  CHARLEY IS MY DARLING (1940). *Novel.*
  A HOUSE OF CHILDREN (1941). *Novel.*
  THE CASE FOR AFRICAN FREEDOM (1941). *Political Science.*
    Revised edition, 1944.
  HERSELF SURPRISED (1941). *Novel.*
  TO BE A PILGRIM (1942). *Novel.*
  PROCESS OF REAL FREEDOM (1943). *Political Science.*
  THE HORSE'S MOUTH (1944). *Novel.*
  MARCHING SOLDIER (1945). *Poem.*
  THE MOONLIGHT (1946). *Novel.*
  BRITAIN AND WEST AFRICA (1946). *Political Science.*
  THE DRUNKEN SAILOR (1947). *Poem.*
  A FEARFUL JOY (1949). *Novel.*
  PRISONER OF GRACE (1952). *Novel.*
  EXCEPT THE LORD (1953). *Novel.*

Some Critical Studies:
  THE NOVEL SINCE 1939, by Henry Reed (1946).

THE NOVEL, 1945–50, by P. H. Newby (1951).

ADAM INTERNATIONAL REVIEW, Nos. 212–13 (November–December 1950. Issue devoted to Cary, containing articles on the novel by him, his broadcast conversation with Lord David Cecil, ' The Novelist at Work ', and some critical estimates.)

***

Messrs. Michael Joseph publish *Except the Lord* and *Prisoner of Grace* at 12s. 6d. net, and the following novels in the Carfax Edition at half a guinea net each : *Herself Surprised, To Be a Pilgrim, The Horse's Mouth, An American Visitor, Aissa Saved, The African Witch, Mister Johnson, Castle Corner, Charley Is My Darling, A House of Children, The Moonlight,* and *A Fearful Joy.* They publish *The Drunken Sailor* at 6s. net and *Marching Soldier* at 2s. 6d. net.

Messrs. Longmans, Green publish *Britain and West Africa* at 1s. 6d. net.